Eternal Light

An Inspirational book to help with the journey of Spirituality

By Cara Barilla

"When you close your eyes, there is so much more to see."

"Connecting to your soul can sometimes feel foreign."

"The greatest travels sometimes don't require a passport, but simply a quiet haven."

"We are all meant to experience the darkness. Don't be afraid. Just remember even the darkest moments of dusk will eventually meet dawn."

"Sometimes to guide yourself forward, you must guide yourself backwards & from the inside out."

"Peace isn't a state of environment, but a state of mind."

"Sometimes you are given little pieces of heaven in your lifetime; Not for your eyes but your heart to capture it."

"Warmth from the heart is the most valuable universal currency."

"The purest miracles come from your own heart."

"Releasing old routines will begin greater ones."

"I thank my higher self for guiding me through the darkness, suffering and confusion."

"When you are kind, your light is protecting you with love and gratitude."

"Always remember you are a rare source of light; Never be afraid to do things differently."

"You are not just your mind, body and spirit, you are a whole galaxy."

"When I close my eyes, i feel a safe place and thank god for my inner sanctuary."

"Allow your heart, body and gut intuition to guide you through the journey."

"Beauty isn't a physical form; It is a light form which radiates from the heart outward."

"Your body is ready to answer all of your questions."

"Be grateful for your present before it becomes a memory."

"Never add force to progress. You are evolving at the right pace for you."

"Your soul will always take you through many challenges in life; it's up to you to guide yourself through to different life patterns."

"We are all connected in this plane; how we know is how we treat each other."

"Life is a mess; As is a masterpiece."

"Yes, it's important to live in the present. But to be grateful for your past is creating a blissful future."

"When we truly accept our light, we are embracing our unique spirit."

"Sweetness is not disingenuous. It is a natural response to a nurturer."

"There is no search for a happy life, you make it from within."

"Your words are the physical forms of tomorrow."

"The only way you can forgive yourself is to forgive others."

"We all evolve differently; Try not to look around at progression. The true progression is within."

"Notice the light in your soul when you feel something that excites you."

"You are never too old to start something new, as you have a soul that is eternal."

"People who share the same frequency in life can create the most powerful experiences. Some might call this magic."

"Remember, no-one can ever replace your heart."

"There's a miracle in each day; Whether it be a tiny smile, good luck or simply the day itself."

"Kindness is eternal bliss."

"When you can see the peace amid the chaos;
You've found your inner temple."

"When you let go of all your expectations you will see that you are already fulfilled."

"Love can be found in a smile, a laugh and a thank you."

"Feel nurture within your soul through sun, wind, waves and light."

"Your soul has its own language that only our subconscious understands."

"You will soon see that your eyes gather dreams and your spirit transforms them into physical form."

"Your soul gives you signs every day; Allowing your body to receive them is another soul challenge."

"Say YES to your heart. For it holds the single map for your soul's journey."

"You have complete power over your life journey and you can use your inner light to have complete control over your thoughts."

"Don't forget to talk to your higher self. Loving your inner voice can be more healing and understanding to your troubles than anyone else."

"Let your inner light shine through any darkness along the way."

"Soul recognition is when people who may have just met, feel they were never strangers, but feel reunited."

"People can influence you with their energy whether it be good or bad with only your consent."

"You are a creator made up of infinite energy ready to create infinite circumstances."

"I ask my higher self to protect me with light, protection and a clear pathway."

"A kind heart will always reveal eyes that will light up the universe."

"Your higher self has provided you with the life you can endure; Whether it's full of challenges or not, you are forever guided."

"Never walk away from your heart; whether your heart is with another passion or person"

"Always look for signs when your soul wants to keep you on the right path; This may mean guiding yourself out of your comfort zone."

"Warmth in a human is what makes our soul thrive; Without it we are cold and merely functioning from something or someone else."

"Sometimes it's best to quiet the mind and allow your soul to take the lead."

"When you live in mindfulness of energy, frequency and vibration you can create your universe."

"A smile, warm eye contact and a hug are things that our soul can take anywhere and anytime."

"The best of your surroundings will allow your soul to grow and to shine light onto others."

"A hungry soul will express its longing throughout all forms of the physical body."

"Allow the portals of thought to embrace your present and create your unique future."

"Resentment keeps us frozen in a dark place;
Forgiveness lifts us high to the light."

"The beauty of patience can paint a beautiful painting when left alone; Sit back, wait and view the art that will unfold."

"Be patient; Don't be disappointed, as something greater will come to you. The magic of Divine timing will send you what you need at the right time."

"Things you do either give you energy or drain your energy. Choose carefully."

"God will always send you many soul challenges;
This will test you for soul ascension."

"This life of creation is to simply create; And this life of living is to simply live."

"Sometimes being alone is your soul's way of growing and learning."

"Some thoughts are meant to pass you by.. without giving it too much energy whether they may be good or bad. When you simply choose which thoughts to keep and which thoughts deserve your energy, this is manifesting your future."

"It's hard to look for happiness in the same place you lost it."

"Recycling thoughts will recycle your current situation."

"You will always be one single thought away from a whole new life path."

"Everything In life is temporary. The only thing that lasts forever is what you hold in your heart."

"Give yourself nurture by doing something today that your future self will thank you for."

"It's okay to stop and change your path. We are not all meant to be moving predictably in life. Sometimes going forward also means moving backwards."

"Smile more; Because the only person who has your soul is you."

"Think less; And feel more."

"Be present; As we only have now to create our future."

"Light frequency is contagious. Be careful how you use your power."

"Give more; Because no-one else has your heart."

"Expect less; And you will rarely be disappointed."

"Quality thoughts equals a quality life. What does quality truly mean to you?"

"Walk with those who always show you a new perspective on life; these are doors leading us to never-ending dimensions."

"Show the world what your heart is made of."

"Cycles will always repeat itself only until you've learned it's hidden life lesson."

"We are non-physical light sources in physical gifts. Play create and use this physical world to give pure gifts to others."

"Beginnings are magical; as they are bright new blank canvases for you to paint your perfect masterpiece."

"Sometimes the simplest things in life are more than enough."

"The universe will never know if you have parted with someone physically in this world. As the mind and heart tell the universe otherwise."

"When you are loved you are forever abundant."

"The mind will look for meaning, the heart will feel an ache for meaning & the soul drifts where it needs to be."

"Your frequency will always create your reality."

"When you believe in yourself you belong to your own universe."

"In order to change your outer world, you must change your inner world."

"No-one else can be you. Let your uniqueness be your superpower and shine your unique light."

"The more you evolve and shift to bright new circumstances in life, comes sacrifices and endings of things that no longer serve your energy."

"In order to rise up to a new state of consciousness; You must allow yourself to feel you deserve to rise up from your old self and your old ways."

"You will always have someone who supports you; Whether you know it or not."

"When we embrace and accept the emotions around us whether good or bad, we are in present."

"Happiness is never a destination. It is the feeling you feel now. The gift of acceptance you give to your presence."

"Sometimes your soul will guide you through very hard times, simply so your soul can experience very hard times."

"When you are in harmony with the world that is the rhythm of peace."

"When you truly believe you have infinite energy, you will be able to create more."

"I allow my higher self to contact me through my 5 senses and guide me through pure intuition."

"Sometimes journaling to yourself can later open up new messages that only your soul can read."

"If you are truly humble, you will never know you are."

"Always take time to feed your soul. Whether it is through laughter, music, prayer, creation, love and play; Your soul always knows the right kind of healing it needs."

"You are an aspect of the universe."

"To be true to your soul, you may have to walk away from certain situations to purely protect yourself. Let the light guide you and always follow your trusting instincts."

"Sometimes you can find light in the darkest of places."

"Saying no to toxic environments may be hard, though when you have released it all, you will feel you are where you are meant to be."

"Allowing your soul to wander is one of the most powerful things you can do. As you belong to freedom. Let your energy flow where it is meant to be without any restrictions."

"When you accept that you cannot please everyone and accept that not everyone will ever understand you will be mind settling."

"Life will forever travel in cycles; New destinations, energies and circumstances."

"Letting go of past thoughts of negativity is forever soul nurturing."

"When we accept that we cannot catch our dreams right now and purely embrace the present, is when you will manifest your dreams."

"You are born to heal, create and love."

"You won't be rewarded in heaven for a clean house; But a clean heart."

"Being humble isn't knowing you are humble;
But an oblivious & natural way of life."

"Letting go of toxic energies by choice will naturally bring in positive light energy."

"It's okay to protect your energy by pausing and not making a move."

"Reminiscing into your positive memories will allow you to embrace the positive present."

"Whenever you close your eyes, you can enter whatever reality you create in your mind. This will manifest itself into reality."

"Never feel guilty for protecting yourself and your loved ones from negative energy."

"Allow your intuition to be your counsellor. Ask questions and your body will answer."

"You can't place an age on wisdom."

"Remember to not feed toxic energy; When it arrives, be still and let it pass as it doesn't belong to you."

"The gateway to a new life is to change your perspective."

"Positive change may not look positive at all."

"The soul's power is infinite."

"Breathe, let go of the past and enjoy the present of presence."

"Remember you are your own power source; When you try and give negative energy to others you are building it up within yourself too."

"Learn to shift your thoughts differently and simply each day; From thinking of new positive thoughts to new ways of accepting the uncontrollable."

"You will open the new door to happiness when you stop looking for the key; And realising you are the key."

"Walk away when you don't feel comfortable. Your intuition never lies."

"Don't forget where your energy source comes from. Not from fear but from pure light. The choice is yours to decide where to recycle your energy."

"Life's struggles can help you search inwards;
Life's rewards can help you give outwards."

"A healer is a believer."

"You can learn something new each day and you can create something new each day; Including miracles.. whether they are for yourself or gifted to someone else."

"Your inner light wants to guide you. Open your heart and embrace your true self to become alight."

"The answer is outside your comfort zone."

"Allow yourself to accept the new cycle of life; It will only bring in things that will nurture your souls longing."

"Very little is needed for self-happiness."

"Allow your ears to hear love."

"Where is your soul travelling to? Close your eyes and visualise your deepest dreams."

"Hope is in the heart."

"Protecting your soul is just as important as giving a little piece of your soul to someone else."

"Thank you for giving me a soul challenge; For it has helped me become the person I am today."

"We are all imperfect and all a reflection of each other."

"We are all made up of unique energy and it is important to know that we cannot be like any other soul."

"Our light is designed to illuminate through our unique pathway. To lighten up the darkness and to shine bright on new directions for only our soul to see ."

"Your good deeds are seen and will create a karmic transformation."

"You are nearly there. What is taking so long you say? The protective force field; Some May call it the "Comfort Zone". Break out and you can create anything."

"Your soul feeds off the energy of your surrounds. Whether light or dark."

"It's the universal rule that you are always going to be loved."

"You always have permission to change your present."

"It's okay if they don't understand you. You were meant to be living in different dimensions."

"I thank my angels for guiding me safely to where I need to be right now in my frequency."

"When we feel love, we are experiencing a pure instant connection to our true source."

"Before you go to sleep in your bed at home;
Always remember to be grateful for going to
sleep in your bed at home."

"I trust the power of air to flow my light energy to the right path."

"Hope is a magical ingredient."

"Living in light is a choice."

"I thank my angels, guardians and loved ones for bringing me positive light each day to help me grow, heal and protect."

"When you believe you are protected by something great, believe yourself because you certainly are."

"Life is a playing-field of love, heartbreak and magic."

"Some people come into this world to bring the light, follow the light or to be the light."

"Quite simply when you align your present to the frequency you want; That's what you'll receive."

"You are magic. You can create anything you want. Believe and it will appear."

"I ask my higher self to protect my greater energy field from anything negative and heal it with the light of god."

"I trust the power of fire to bring light and passion into my life."

"Bringing joy to an event is more valuable than the event itself."

"Always look up to see your endless possibilities. When you look down only see how far you've risen."

"When you walk into the room your energy will always speak before you do."

"I thank god for keeping my family safe and happy. I am grateful for my soul's ascension."

"Shifting energy is as possible as it is impossible."

"You are a protector. You naturally protect your soul's main energy source. Your higher self."

"When you trust in the divine light you are surrendering to yourself and letting go of fear."

"When you believe, you can manifest, trust, heal and create."

"A strong heart under bright light is a walking miracle."

"Your inner light will guide you forever."

"I trust the power of water to cleanse heal and balance my emotions."

"Our 5 senses are gateways to our higher self. Try to give and receive back to yourself."

"Channel your inner light worker. Allow yourself to act in pure light of service to others; For this is angelic work."

"Energy of light brings new pathways for angels to walk."

"Self-sacrifice can heal you in ways you could never imagine."

"Life will always shift its energy. Never expect for things to stay the same."

"Allow your higher self to release ego. When you live with your true spirit, you will be eternally at satisfaction."

"Some people will come into your energy to shift, heal or guide you."

"You lived that experience to feel that unique emotion. Don't regret this but learn and allow yourself to guide yourself through a lighter path."

"When we forgive others, we are allowing other old energy to forgive us back."

"Following the cycle of evolvement is nothing to be ashamed of. Reward yourself."

"It's okay to feel guilt. Shift this emotion into kindness and service for others. Your karmic journey still awaits you."

"It's time to see all the broken pieces of your heart become a mosaic masterpiece."

"I thank god for channelling my thoughts to memories of reflection. I now see where I must flow my energy and my actions in light."

"I trust the earths soil to ground me as I heal my toxins away."

"You are divine light. Shed your light onto those that need to heal and shine."

"And the unknown will always be the most beautiful creation by god."

"God bless you. You are a creator of light. You are always loved. And will always love. Eternally."